D1377173

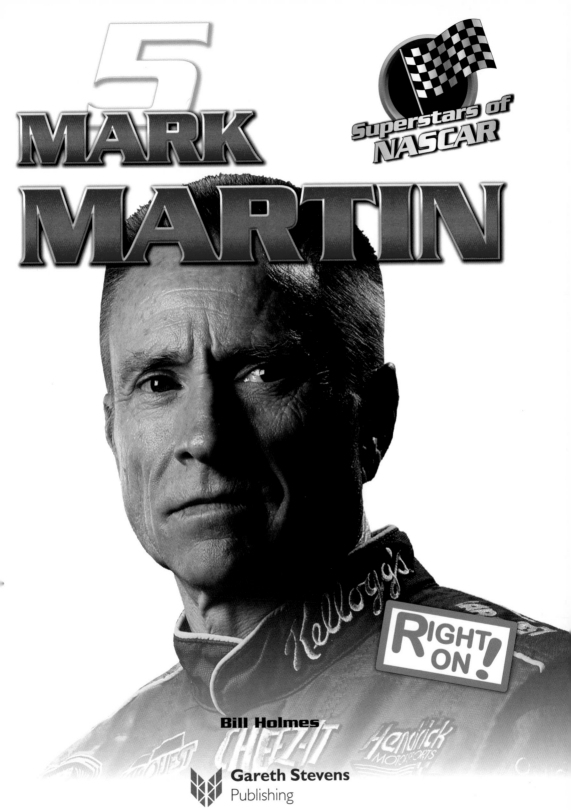

5
MARK
MARTIN

Superstars of NASCAR

RIGHT ON!

Bill Holmes

Gareth Stevens
Publishing

Please visit our Web site, www.garethstevens.com. For a free color catalog of all our high-quality books, call toll free 1-800-542-2595 or fax 1-877-542-2596.

Library of Congress Cataloging-in-Publication Data

Mark Martin / Bill Holmes.
     p. cm. — (Superstars of NASCAR)
   Includes index.
   ISBN 978-1-4339-3966-2 (pbk.)
   ISBN 978-1-4339-3967-9 (6-pack)
   ISBN 978-1-4339-3965-5 (library binding)
   1. Martin, Mark, 1959—Juvenile literature. 2. Automobile racing drivers—United States—Biography—Juvenile literature. I. Title.
   GV1032.M36H65 2010
   796.72092 dc22
   [B]
                                        2010007391

First Edition

Published in 2011 by
Gareth Stevens Publishing
111 East 14th Street, Suite 349
New York, NY 10003

Designer: Michael J. Flynn
Editor: Mary Ann Hoffman

Photo credits: Cover (Mark Martin), pp. 1, 7, 23 Rusty Jarrett/Getty Images; cover, pp. 4, 6, 8, 10, 12, 16, 18, 20, 22, 24, 28 (background on all) Shutterstock.com; p. 5 Stephen Dunn/Getty Images; pp. 9, 17 Todd Warshaw/Getty Images; pp. 11, 14–15 Darrell Ingham/Getty Images; p. 13 Focus On Sports/Getty Images; p. 19 David Taylor/Getty Images; p. 21 Dozier Mobley/Getty Images; pp. 25, 26–27 RacingOne/ISC Archives/Getty Images; p. 29 John Harrelson/Getty Images.

Printed in the United States of America

CPSIA compliance information: Batch #CS10GS: For further information contact Gareth Stevens, New York, New York at 1-800-542-2595.

Contents

A Winner

Mark Martin is a famous NASCAR Sprint Cup Series driver. He has raced in NASCAR for more than 25 years! He has won many races!

5

Winning Early

Mark Martin was born in Arkansas on January 9, 1959. He started racing as a teenager. He raced on dirt tracks.

While still a teenager, Mark began racing all over the country. He was named ASA Rookie of the Year when he was just 18.

Mark Martin

Mark was a very good racer in the ASA. He won three championships in a row!

11

NASCAR

In 1981, Mark decided to race in the top stock car racing series. He began racing in NASCAR.

In the NASCAR Sprint Cup Series, Mark had two top-10 finishes his first year. He had eight top-10 finishes his second year.

A Return to ASA

In NASCAR, Mark raced for several different owners. In 1984, he decided to return to the ASA.

Two years later, Mark Martin won the ASA Championship for the fourth time.

The Nationwide Series

In 1988, NASCAR team owner Jack Roush noticed Mark's driving skill. Mark returned to NASCAR to drive for Roush in the Nationwide Series.

Jack Roush   Mark Martin

Mark drove the number 6 car for Roush for 19 years! It is the longest an owner and driver have worked together in the history of NASCAR.

Winning a Cup Race

Mark Martin won his first Sprint Cup race in 1989. He was named NASCAR Driver of the Year.

Mark Martin

In 1994, Mark won the International Race of Champions (IROC). This race has the best drivers from different kinds of car racing. Mark won the IROC four more times!

Mark Martin has been a successful NASCAR racer. In 2009, he became one of only four NASCAR drivers to win a Sprint Cup race after turning 50!

Timeline

1959 Mark is born in Arkansas.

1977 Mark is named Rookie of the Year in the ASA.

1981 Mark begins racing in NASCAR.

1984 Mark returns to the ASA.

1988 Mark returns to NASCAR.

1989 Mark wins his first NASCAR Sprint Cup race.

1994 Mark wins his first IROC.

2009 Mark wins a Sprint Cup race after turning 50.

For More Information

Books:

Mello, Tara Baukus. *Mark Martin.* New York, NY: Chelsea
House, 2008.

Robinson, Tim. *Mark Martin: Master Behind the Wheel.*
Berkeley Heights, NJ: Enslow Publishers, 2008.

Web Sites:

Mark Martin Biography
nascar.suite101.com/article.cfm/mark_martin_biography

NASCAR.com: Mark Martin
www.nascar.com/drivers/dps/mmartin00/cup/index.html

Publisher's note to educators and parents: Our editors have carefully reviewed these Web sites to
ensure that they are suitable for students. Many Web sites change frequently, however, and we cannot
guarantee that a site's future contents will continue to meet our high standards of quality and educational
value. Be advised that students should be closely supervised whenever they access the Internet.

Glossary

ASA: the American Speed Association, which is an official racing series

championship: a series of races to decide a winner

international: having to do with two or more countries

Nationwide Series: a NASCAR racing series that is one level below the Sprint Cup Series

rookie: a person in their first year of a sport

Sprint Cup Series: the top racing series of NASCAR

Index